JONAH

*A Man, A Plan,
A Fish, A Plant*

JIM CARNS

LUCIDBOOKS

Jonah: A Man, a Plan, a Fish, a Plant

Copyright © 2026 by Jim Carns

Published by Lucid Books in Houston, TX
www.LucidBooks.com

Unless otherwise indicated, Scripture quotations are taken from the Lexham English Bible (LEB) (copyright © 2012 by Lexham Press, Bellingham, WA). Used by permission. All rights reserved.

ISBN: 978-1-63296-915-6
eISBN: 978-1-63296-916-3

Special sales: Most Lucid Books titles are available in special quantity discounts. Custom imprinting or excerpting can also be done to fit special needs. Contact Lucid Books at Info@LucidBooks.com.

To my wife, Ashley, for loving me.

JONAH

INTRODUCTION

The choice of one man to disobey God brought many to follow God. This book is about lost battles and a triumphant victory, followed by a bitter end. To understand the full intention of Jonah is to try to grasp the ill intentions of one man who wants to disobey God because of his own will and desire for the end of others. Working toward understanding God, Nineveh, and Jonah is quite the task that may feel as though we will not see an end or have a complete understanding.

Nineveh was known to be evil. Jonah was a known prophet who was sent by God, and God had a plan that worked out perfectly. We will see the evil that came from Nineveh, the necessity of Jonah's selfishness, the repentance of a great city, and the demise of a prophet. This is not our world, and our choices do not matter. And God's will—it will be done. That is the conversation Jonah should have had with himself before he decided to run. Before you say, "Well, that is obvious," ask yourself how many times you have decided to go against what you knew was right. Or how many times did you know what God wanted to do through you but you decided you did not want to follow that plan or take that path?

CHAPTER 1

1:1–2

And the word of Yahweh came to Jonah the son of Amittai, saying, "Get up! Go to the great city Nineveh and cry out against her, because their evil has come up before me."

We meet Jonah at the beginning of his book. His father, Amittai, is included to make it known that we are talking about a specific person at a particular time. Jonah was a prophet of Yahweh, a position held in high regard by all from his time, today, and for days to come. Knowing that Yahweh directly called Jonah to go to the great city of Nineveh shows that there should be great things to come for Jonah and Nineveh. Jonah, like all of us who are Christ-followers, was given specific direction on what he was to do with his life. This direction was given to him in verse two of chapter one. Yahweh said "Get up! Go to the great city Nineveh and cry out against her, because their evil has come up *before me.*" This was given to Jonah with exclamation showing that there was urgency in what Jonah was to do for Nineveh. The urgency was added because of the evil of the great city of Nineveh. A whole city was to be destroyed since there was great evil throughout the great city with no remorse. The evil seen in Sodom and Gomorrah comes to mind when we ponder the evil that Nineveh was participating in. When you were called by Yahweh, how excited were you to go where He directed?

Verse two is as direct as it comes. If I heard from Yahweh with that direct of a conversation, that is what I would do because Yahweh came to me specifically with a plan and a goal. To hear the direction is easy, but to follow through with it is where difficulty and even doubt come into play. It is difficult to change, and it is difficult to do something we did not want to do or do not want to do today. It is difficult to go to a place we are not familiar with and where we believe we are not wanted. Then there is the doubt we fight with regularly. Am I really the one Yahweh wants to send? Am I prepared for what is to come, whether it is good or bad? Does Yahweh really want me to say that to them? All these questions are valid questions, but the reality is that we need to make sure we are not asking questions with the goal of saying no to any of them. Saying no is finding our way to justify not doing what Yahweh has told us to do. Are our answers based on selfish goals and desires? When we say no for any reason, our selfishness shows and puts us in a place of disobedience.

At the end of these first two verses of Jonah, we see that Yahweh made a plan and gave direction, and Jonah said no.

Why did Jonah say no? There are many speculations. Maybe he did not like Nineveh because of how violent they were to him or his family. Or maybe he knew they were evil and was therefore afraid for his life. There are many potential reasons he was trying to not follow Yahweh's direct plan, but none of them are important. The only thing that is important is that Jonah decided to disobey Yahweh and run another direction.

1:3

But Jonah set out to flee toward Tarshish from the presence of Yahweh. And he went down to Joppa and found a merchant ship going to Tarshish, and paid her fare, and went on board her to go with them toward Tarshish from the presence of Yahweh.

Jonah saying no is where we find ourselves in the following verses. Not only did Jonah attempt to flee but he was working on going 2,500 miles from the location he needed to be according to Yahweh's plan. Jonah was not only trying to flee from Nineveh, but he was trying to flee from the face of Yahweh. Because Jonah regularly talked to Yahweh, he knew it would take more than just a walk to hide from Yahweh. How far have you gone to run from your obligations? Did you go to another state or country, or are you hiding in porn, drugs, and alcohol?

Our potential hero decides to run in the opposite direction—not just the opposite direction but thousands of miles away from the place Yahweh specifically told Jonah to go. It is interesting to see that he set out toward Tarshish to try to get away from the face of Yahweh. Don't you think he would have realized that he cannot run from Yahweh? Jonah is a prophet and has direct communication with Yahweh, yet he decides to attempt to run. Yes, *attempt* is the correct word as we will soon see the results of his attempt. Jonah paid for the fare to run, which will prove to be the price he did not want to pay for the results he did not want. When you decided to run from the words and face of God, how far did you get with *your* plan? How successful were you at reaching *your* planned destination?

1:4

And Yahweh hurled a great wind upon the sea, and it was a great storm on the sea, and the merchant ship was in danger of breaking up.

As we will see, there are many correlations to our lives and Jonah's life based on his poor decision and ours. In verse four we see that because of Jonah's poor decision, Yahweh sent a storm to come upon the sea where Jonah was, causing the mariners to fear death when they were just trying to get their jobs done. Because of this act of disobedience, how many people had their lives in danger because of Jonah's running from Yahweh? We do not know that number. And how many people have problems in their lives because of decisions you have made? Those decisions are not just ones for today but ones of time past. How many people were afraid for their lives or livelihoods because of things you have said or done that were not to be done or said by anyone, especially you? Though these questions may seem rhetorical, they are things you need to take into consideration as you make decisions to disobey Yahweh.

Diving deeper into verse four of chapter one, we need to understand what was about to happen and what happened to the mariners. The mariners' plan was a trip to Tarshish. Jonah's plan was a man escaping, and Yahweh's plan was ignored. When Yahweh is ignored, there are consequences. Yahweh was already angry with Nineveh, and Jonah made it worse by ignoring a direct command with specific instructions.

Yahweh sent a great storm. A storm is one conversation, but a great storm from Yahweh is nothing to be trifled with. A great storm while on land is typically something that will not take away your life; however, when you are at sea, there is no control of what is happening or what will happen because there is no actual shelter and nothing firm to stand on or hide under. Because Yahweh hurled a great wind, it shows that this was not a natural occurrence but was supernatural. The wind was so great that the merchant ship was in danger of breaking up, taking away any potential security the mariners felt they had. Those who are not seagoing people do not comprehend the danger they must have felt. Those who do not have potentially life-changing events do not know what this is about. Those who have lived through life-changing events and great "storms" can attempt to explain their situation, usually without success. But to understand if you were not there is not easy. The listener may have had similar experiences but they were never the same.

1:5

And the mariners were afraid, and each cried out to his god. And they threw the contents that were in the merchant ship into the sea to lighten it for them. And meanwhile Jonah went down into the hold of the vessel and lay down and fell asleep.

Going to verse five, we see that there was enough going wrong that the mariners were crying out to their gods. As they prayed to their gods, nothing happened because their gods were nothing. We see them going on a crash diet or a weight loss program so they do not crash; either way, they fear the inevitable crash. Therefore, they threw away everything they had paid for or were paid to transport to the city of Tarshish. Fear of loss of life and actual loss of money, though different in many ways, carry similarities. Loss of money may often mean loss of life; loss of life is a finality that no one wants but knows is coming eventually.

While the mariners were fearing for their lives and praying the best way they know how, Jonah made his bed and lay in it, literally and figuratively. Finding a way to rest in times of desperation is difficult unless you put your trust in who is in charge—Yahweh. Knowing that Jonah was sleeping tells us that he knew who was in charge. Jonah was not acting like it mattered who was in charge, based on his path and his direction in not following Yahweh. I'm not saying that we should sleep in times of trouble because sometimes that is the best idea. This verse shows that Jonah's intention was to hide until there was nothing left to do but die in the wreckage of the ship. Seeing that Jonah was okay with dying is disheartening. He did not care about the lives of those around him. We see this based on running from Nineveh and that he is sleeping when the ship is going to be going down in the storm from Yahweh. Who are you willing to take down with you—your spouse, your kids, your parents, or your church?

Ponder this moment on the ship. Because of one man attempting to run from Yahweh, a whole ship, crew, and items on the ship were going to perish. One man decided that because of his unwillingness to follow Yahweh, many will perish. This is not something that anyone should be doing at any time. Jonah did not care about the lives of those around him. He just did not want to go to Nineveh where Yahweh had directed him to go. Proverbs 3:5–6 says, "*Trust Yahweh* with all your heart; do not lean toward your own understanding. In all your ways acknowledge him, and he will straighten your paths." Where Jonah messed up according to these verses is that he leaned on his own understanding and made his own path rather crooked. But as we will soon discover, Yahweh straightened his path for him.

Before we continue, we need to understand more deeply the path Jonah could have chosen versus the path he took. Jonah could have gone straight to Nineveh. He would have been there quickly, done what was required, and then returned home. But he did not choose the easy path; he chose the one that put the lives of many at risk, including his own. At what point of Jonah's adventure should he have turned back? At what point of your adventure should you turn back? If you see that point, time, or place when you should turn back, then you are able now to stop where you are and turn back. Yahweh does love, He does forgive, and we need to do our part to follow His plan with intention.

1:6

And the captain of the ship approached him and said to him, "Why are you sound asleep? Get up! Call on your god! Perhaps your god will take notice of us and we won't perish!"

The captain found Jonah. The captain wanted Jonah and everyone else to save the ship and all that was on it. Did Yahweh send the captain to find Jonah? Yahweh's plan was to continue getting Jonah on the right path. The captain does not know that Jonah follows Yahweh, God, as much as he knows there is a god out there who he believes will help them with what is going wrong on the sea. "Why are you *sound asleep?*" That was the question the captain asked Jonah, but I ask that of you. Why are you sleeping? Why are you not following Yahweh with His direction for your life? Sleeping for Jonah was literal sleep that he needed for what was to come. Sleeping for us is doing what we are not called to do. It's wasting time fighting Yahweh by having a career that is not what we were directed to do but what we want to do because of our own selfish desires, excuses, and justifications.

Or maybe you are busy doing the Lord's "work" in a church but not the work the Lord has for you.

"Get up!" This is not the first time Jonah was told to get up and do something. First was Yahweh, and now it was the captain. Get up is a theme here. Jonah had to get up for Yahweh, and now he must get up for the captain. How many times do you need to hear "get up" before you actually get up? It should only take one time. More than one time is sin because we are disobeying Yahweh's direction. "Call on your god!" the captain said, not knowing that Jonah was running from his god. The captain is telling Jonah to do what will fix this situation. It could have all gone away much faster. If Jonah had not made his own plan, the storm would not have even come upon them.

1:7

And they said to one another, "Come, let us cast lots so that we may know on whose account this disaster has come on us!" And they cast lots, and the lot fell on Jonah.

When is the last time you gambled to find an answer? We can go as far as to say, when did you flip a coin to have a yes or no answer? Eeny, meeny, miny, moe? My guess is not many times can you remember participating in casting lots to find truth. In verse seven, we find that happening. The mariners did not want to just throw Jonah overboard since they did not want to remove the one who brought the storm without further clarification on who it was and what to do with them. The mariners knew it was something evil, and they knew something had to be done with the evil and the one who brought the evil.

We know from the previous verses that Jonah is the issue. If I am Jonah, I have two thoughts. If this was not me, maybe the cast lot will not fall on me. Or let's get this over with because it is me, and we just need to move forward. We do not have a reference as to how many times they cast the die or if they did not know who it was, but this must have been like waiting for the results on a test that is life or death. As the cast lots fell on Jonah, a sigh of relief fell on the hearts and minds of the rest of the individuals on the ship that is still being tossed because of the wind from Yahweh.

1:8

So they said to him, "Please tell us whoever is responsible that this disaster has come upon us! What is your occupation? And from where do you come? What is your country? And from which people are you?"

The questions came flooding in like the wind that was causing the waters to crash down upon them. We desire to know all that is needed and even more. We desire to name things. This desire is from Adam when he was called to name all things on earth. Naming things is what gives us references to what we want and need to know for further information and investigation. Now that the mariners know who brought this upon them, they have much more they want to know.

The mariners sought understanding of the situation to its fullest with four questions that should tell them all they needed to know. They needed to know what Jonah did as his occupation; an occupation gives insight into a person's education. That was important to understand because it would further their understanding of what needed to be done to move on from this time of distress. "From where do you come?" Other potential answers that you get from that are who or what you are running from. Do the mariners need to worry about an army coming after them, even when Jonah has been removed from their presence? Is Jonah's god the real god? Will God condemn them because they helped Jonah? Their fear could have been because they did not want God to chase after them even though they were unaware of Jonah's plan to run. All they knew is that he wanted to go to Tarshish.

"What is your country?" Why is that important? Why does it matter? There are a few reasons it matters. It could be because they know some places were known for being evil; for example, Nineveh. Where you are from tells your story as well. Are you from a loved town or a town that was full of no-good people? If Jonah was from a hated place, that may bring more clarity to the reason for their calamity. Knowing where someone is from also helps you potentially see the truth and the context of who the person is. Though this is not always the case, we do hold opinions about people based on where they are from. That should not be the case, but often it is. Do you want to be looked down upon because you are from the same town as one that has caused much evil? I say no. Then we need to be sure that we are not doing this to others as we learn where they are from.

"And from which people are you?" That seems like it may be redundant. How many ways can we ask someone who they are? Just because you are from the United States of America, you may not be of the people of America. There are many who are originally from another country such as China, and they would be their people, but they are from America because that is where they live. The culture some-one lives in can tell you another factor of the person you are trying to understand.

1:9

And he said to them, "I am a Hebrew, and I fear Yahweh, the God of heaven, who made the sea and the dry land."

Jonah replies to all the questions with one sentence, though each of those questions deserves an answer by them-selves. To be able to use one sentence to tell all is a great lead into the rest of the conversation. One sentence tells you who you are perishing with and who is bringing the thunder. "I am a Hebrew" tells quite a bit in those four words. Jonah expressed his nationality, his religion, and his people. There are not many statements that can be used to answer so many questions in one fast moment. To be an American says our country, but each state in America has its own culture, creed, and lifestyle. To say you are an American, you still need to say north or south, east or west, Bible Belt or tornado alley, and many other descriptions before you have the answer from the statement "I am an American."

The next phrase that he says is "I fear Yahweh." Hearing that without more context could have been enough information to set all on the right path. They were in a time of great fear, the kind of fear that is often followed by death. Jonah fears Yahweh more than the fear of the sea engulfing them. The fear of the moment is such that no one would expect anyone to be able to express more fear of anyone or anything, yet Jonah fears Yahweh more. Do you fear Yahweh? Do you know what He could do if you provoke Him enough? Not only does Jonah say Yahweh, but he shares that He is the God of heaven. The God of heaven is something that is understood to be above all, not just what we can see but what is unseen also. He is the God of heaven where the rain and wind come from as well as the heat from the sun and the light of the moon and stars.

Jonah continues to speak of God, the creator of the sea and dry land. God created the place they wanted to be as well as the place where they were. If God can create this place, then He can control and even destroy this place and that place. Jonah admitted that Yahweh is the one who brought all this upon them because he made the wrong decision. As the mariners learned of Yahweh being the creator of the sea, surely they realized the sea is all things to them. The sea is their food, their livelihood, and their ability to travel. The sea is their all. Dry land was where they wanted to be at that time because the sea was crashing down upon them. The land was where their family was, where they could feel secure. Jonah worshiped the God who created the place they wanted to be. When we understand who we are fighting against, we need to understand whether we can win the fight or lose. When fighting God who created all, do you think you have a chance at winning? Are you fighting because you want to rebel or because you are afraid of the results of following God?

1:10

Then the men were greatly afraid, and they said to him, "What is this you have done?" because they knew that he was fleeing from the presence of Yahweh (because he had told them).

The men were already afraid that their lives were at risk of being lost at sea. Now they were greatly afraid. How do you go from afraid to greatly afraid? You learn that your life may end in hell because Yahweh, the creator of all things, is the one who is angry. "What did you do?" What evil could Jonah have done to cause this distress on them all? What egregious act was he hiding from that other lives may perish? Why was he not facing his wrongs and seeking to repent?

Those are things we need to ask ourselves regularly. We have brought our problems on ourselves, so we need to know what we did wrong. In Jonah's case, we see that he already told them he was running from Yahweh, but they did not have the full scope of what he did wrong to have to run from the presence of Yahweh. Why are you fleeing Yahweh? Why are you not following through with His plan for your life? You know you have something to do for God. And now you need to get out of your "boat" and get back into the presence of Yahweh.

1:11

So they said to him, "What shall we do to you so that the sea may quiet down for us?" because the sea was growing more and more tempestuous.

Here we are. We have learned why the sea was so violent. We have learned who brought this upon them. Now how do we deal with this? What should we do with the ones who cause us so much turmoil that we must seek out the answer from Yahweh by way of casting lots? Do you have someone who is causing you issues? Is there someone in your life you need to remove? You need to be asking this question: "What shall we do to you so that my life is full of God and not distractions again?" Have you found that life continues to get worse the longer you have the wrong person or persons in your life? The sea was growing more and more tempestuous. It was bad enough that they were afraid, and now they are greatly afraid because the sea continued to increasingly bear down on them. The destruction of having the wrong person on their ship had proved to be so much more than they could endure. They must solve the problem or face imminent doom.

1:12

And he said to them, "Pick me up and hurl me into the sea so that the sea may quiet down for you, because I know that on account of me this great storm has come upon you all."

Jonah has a plan. Though it appears to not be a great plan, it is a plan nonetheless. Jonah's plan is to commit what he thought was assisted suicide. Jonah wanted to be thrown into the sea instead of casting himself into the sea. Having them do the casting would cause the men to be guilty of killing him instead of Jonah solving their problems himself. "Pick me up." In other words, I cannot do this myself; this task must be done by someone else.

"Hurl me into the sea." Throw me as far as you can into the sea as in don't let me hit the ship on my way down while it is tossing about in the tempestuous sea. Jonah follows this up with if you do this, you will be saved. The mariners hear if you kill me you will live. That does not make sense to anyone because with death is more death since they're perceived as murderers. Hearing that if Jonah is thrown over they will have a chance to live makes them say let's get throwing. Grab his legs, and I will grab his arms. But do you really think you could be one of the ones to throw him overboard to the probable demise of his life? Thankfully, you will only know if you are put in that position. Pray that you never have to make that decision.

Imagine finding the reason for the problem going on in your life but your life does not get better because you do not want to let that problem go. It might be friends, habits, family, or anything else that is your idol. That is not to say that Jonah was their idol, but it is to say that they knew what was going on. Knowing what is causing the problem and doing something about it is not easy, but it is necessary. When we let evil in because we are selfish and do not want to do what God asks of us, there needs to be expectations of correcting behavior from God to us.

Here are the next questions you need to ask: Will the sea really calm down? Will my life be saved because of this? Will ending of his life save mine? I do not know that I could end someone's life just to save mine. But let's get back to the sea quieting down because of this. If this is the plan, then this is the path that needs to happen. Jonah's admitting that he is the reason for the storm is a great way to start the process. Admitting when we sin is a good way to end our desire to sin. Seeking help is what we need to work out our sins with the plan of leaving them behind. Was Jonah looking for help to not sin anymore or not live anymore? He said it was because of him that these evil things were happening. Can you say that and mean it with the intention of stopping evil from happening to others?

Wanting to end evil for others is a great way to live. Knowing what I need to do differently is what I need to focus on. We are not always self-aware of our evil that affects others' lives because we often are not observant of the destruction of others' lives. Jonah does not have the ability to leave out the destruction of others in his thoughts because they are all potentially going down with the ship.

1:13

But the men rowed hard to bring the ship back to the dry land, and they could not do so because the sea was growing more and more tempestuous against them.

With all of this going on, the mariners still decided to attempt to row back to dry land. They knew the problem, they knew who caused it, and they knew how to solve the problem, yet they still tried not to do what was necessary to stop the storm. And I still want to keep that person who takes me down the path to evil in my life. I do not want to remove that sin I enjoy so much from my life, even though it hurts me physically and emotionally. I did all I can do, but I did not do what I needed to do: call upon Yahweh. All the efforts I put forth will fail. They will not move me toward safety. They will not direct me to the best place. They will leave me stranded in my own filth and shame. The mariners knew where to find dry land, and they knew where to point the ship. They tried with all they had, but knowing what to do, the direction to go, and the place to be does not mean you will have success.

The sea grew more tempestuous, Yahweh kept hammering them. The sea, also known as consequences, grew because that is what was needed to make the end requirement happen. The sea, or consequences, were relentless because the men did not follow the plan that was given to them. If their intention was to help Jonah, they were actually aiding and abetting him in his willful desire to not follow Yahweh.

Have you helped others live in sin? Have you helped

them continue their path of destruction? Have you made excuses for their actions and not corrected their behavior? Their intentions look correct from the human perspective, but we need to see this from the bigger picture. We need to let the consequences for poor actions and decisions happen. That is how we learn, often and unfortunately. An addict will lose everything and still want the evil that has taken everything because they desire evil more than good. Stop helping those who will not help themselves. They will drag you down a path that is headed to death and destruction. Death here is used as separation. You will be separated from your friends and family because of the addiction of helping the one who is addicted.

1:14

So, they cried out to Yahweh, and they said, "O Yahweh! Please do not let us perish because of this man's life, and do not make us guilty of innocent blood, because you, O Yahweh, did what you wanted."

They cried out. They understood what was next. They sought Yahweh as they cried out. They sought the one who sent the tempestuous storm. When will you seek Yahweh? It's not that He has sent you a storm but that your storm is getting worse, and He is the way to remove it or help you get through it. "O Yahweh!" It sounds like a lament to the one who can save, a cry of help with the intention of following what is their next direction. They continue with their prayer, seeking what they must do to be saved from this storm. They know who has caused the storm to come upon them. The question is what to do with the one who is causing the storm to be in their life. They do not want to be guilty of murder. They knew they had to find the right plan and path. Enough innocent blood is shed, and there is no need for more innocent blood to be shed. Was Jonah innocent? I propose that Jonah was not innocent—not that he killed anyone directly or intentionally but that the Ninevites and the mariners' lives were on the line because of his intention to not follow Yahweh but to go his own way.

The mariners have acknowledged that Yahweh is doing what He wants because He needs Jonah to follow the path he was given. O Yahweh, you will do what you want. What we need to know is how to follow Yahweh without making Him force us to go down the path He needs us to go down. Do you have innocent blood on your hands? Have you not shared Jesus with others? Yahweh's plan will be successful; He will do as He wants. We need to be willing to follow Yahweh and not be pushed in the direction we know we are to go.

1:15

And they picked Jonah up and hurled him into the sea, and the sea ceased from its raging.

One, two, three, and heave ho, off he goes. With all their might, the mariners tossed Jonah into the sea, and Jonah got what he thought was his current wish. Is death the fulfillment of Jonah's desire? Are the mariners now guilty of the death of an innocent man? Will their lives get better? The tension builds as each moment passes. Each moment must have felt like it was forever for Jonah and the mariners. Into the tempestuous sea he goes. Now we see the sea calm from its raging. Has Yahweh been satisfied? All looks great at this point because the sea ceased raging. They followed Yahweh's plan, and all came out well. They listened to Yahweh, and their lives were spared. They followed Yahweh, and what was a problem was now a delight with all back to what would seem normal. That does not mean all your problems will go away immediately when you follow Yahweh, but they will be manageable and not so overwhelming because you will have the creator of all things on your side.

1:16

So, the men feared Yahweh greatly, and they offered a sacrifice to Yahweh and made vows.

The mariners learned of the fierceness of Yahweh and feared Him. And we all must. Fear has many forms—fear of an interview, fear of asking for a first date, fear of asking about something awkward, and so on. But fear of Yahweh was stuck in the hearts and minds of the mariners. They knew fear of death because of the sea, but now they understood who sent this pending doom to them. We're not afraid of the sea until a storm comes, and then we are greatly afraid—not afraid of a god until you know the god that can harm you. Then you are afraid of the God—Yahweh.

Knowing who sent the pending doom tells us who to fear. Now we need to understand how to not be continually afraid. The mariners knew of sacrifices; that was their common way to please the god they worshiped. Naturally, they learn of the God, Yahweh, and realize His power. They know they need to sacrifice to Him. What have you sacrificed for and to Yahweh—your life, your career, your family? What are you willing to give up to follow the God who can send a storm your way. Will you give up your habit, your friends who take you where you need to stay away from, your family who will take you to evil, your anger, or your impatience? Yahweh is the God we need to fear. Yahweh deserves all we have to offer and more. The mariners sacrificed and made vows. A vow is a contract and not a small thing. Today we look at a contract and believe it can be canceled or removed. They did not see a vow as something small or something they could buy out of. It is something that is there for life without question or fail.

Because of Jonah's decision to run from Yahweh and Nineveh, these mariners learned to believe in Yahweh. It was a great thing for them to believe in Yahweh, but at what cost did that happen? Does their belief justify Jonah's action of running from Yahweh? As you ponder that question, think about this: Does going to a bar to witness justify getting drunk? Being drunk is not much of a witness for Christ. It is great that the men believed, sacrificed, and made vows, but would they have done it if someone else had come along or if they did not have to live through a tempestuous storm? Though the end was great for the men's faith, how they got there based on Jonah's decision to disobey Yahweh was not right. It would have been better for them to believe without potential tragedy. But just like you, sometimes that is what it takes for us to believe. O Yahweh! I vow to do as you ask when you ask. I do not want you to have to send a storm for me to follow you.

1:17

And Yahweh provided a large fish to swallow up Jonah, and Jonah was in the belly of the fish three days and three nights.

First there was a storm, and now a fish. What's next? Yahweh provided a large fish. We're not sure what kind of fish it was, but we just need to know that Yahweh provided it. Yahweh was very specific about what He sent to get Jonah's attention. What has been sent your way to get your attention? Was it loss of family, friends, things, safety, security, or health? This seems extreme for Yahweh to get one man's attention. We are all human and stubborn, and some need more direction than others. The large fish swallowed up Jonah, just as our sins and selfish desires swallow us up. We are often too busy with our own plans to follow Yahweh's plans. My time is precious, but eternity needs to be seen as more precious. Therefore, we need to be working for eternity, not for today that is short and fleeting like vapor.

Three days and three nights Jonah was in the belly of the large fish. He was in the depths of his sin at that time—dark, cold, wet, and no help in sight. What is the sin you cannot get out of? What have you done to get in that situation? Was it a text you sent to someone you should not have texted, an inappropriate conversation, or time spent with someone who had nefarious intentions? What have you done to stop the sin that has happened or that will happen if you continue down this path? If the sin is still happening or is about to happen, you have not done enough. That is right. You need to do what is required to stop the wrong from happening.

Here we are with Jonah in the depths of his decisions. Many times he could have turned back. He could have said yes to Yahweh. He could have not sought out the ship. He could have not paid the fare. He could have not boarded the ship. What could you do to not be stuck in the depths of your sin? Every one of your actions has consequences. The consequence is your choice. Will it be positive or negative? Three days and three nights of nothing seems like a short time, but it must have felt like forever to Jonah because of the uncertainty of what was to come.

CHAPTER 2

2:1

And Jonah prayed to Yahweh his God from the belly of the fish.

"And Jonah prayed." That seems to be something he should have been doing all along or, better yet, before he started on his adventure to Tarshish. Praying is a wonderful thing that puts us in the presence of Yahweh. And Jonah finally prayed. When was the last time you prayed before you *had* to pray? When is the last time you sought to be in the presence of God without running away with hopes of not being caught and sent back to where you needed to be? Thankfully, we know that Jonah knows who to pray to—Yahweh his God.

This was a time of many gods, so being specific was important for the time. But is it only important for then? What God do you pray to? Is it television, your smartphone, your friends, your pastor, and more? Yes, your pastor is included on purpose since many will seek the word from their pastor and not the word of the Lord. The word of your pastor can be blown off since it only has the power of a man behind it. The word of the Lord is the word that goes out with power and strength that will sever marrow and bone.

Jonah prayed to Yahweh from a most embarrassing predicament—the belly of a fish, something we are to catch and eat, not be eaten by. Knowing that we did not create fish but are to subdue them is what makes this precarious. What sin has you wrapped up well within it? What situation do you find yourself in that you have to pray for Yahweh to help you out of? You are there because you want to be there, not because you have suddenly found yourself in that situation. I see the fish as the culmination of continually acting sinfully. You cannot get out on your own to get help—not always the help you want or the help you hope for, but it will be help.

2:2

And said, "I called from my distress to Yahweh, and he answered me; from the belly of Sheol I cried for help—you heard my voice."

"I called from my distress"—it seems a bit late in the conversation to be calling anyone when you are wrapped in your sin. You have found yourself in a place that is leading to death in the darkest of ways. How did you get there? Why did you not call out earlier? You are in such a dark place that there is no obvious way out, so you call. Who do you call? Who will help? How will they find you? You call the only one who sees you: Yahweh.

Jonah is in a dark place that has no exit as far as he can see. He is in a place of distress that leads to nothing. Thankfully, he has enough sense about himself to call on the one and only one who can save him—Yahweh. When we call to Yahweh, He will answer. We may not always like the answer, but He will answer. Jonah acknowledges that Yahweh answered in his time of distress.

We have the tendency to look at Jonah and criticize him for not doing this or that, but what about you? When did you call upon Yahweh when you were not in a time of distress? When should Jonah have called upon Yahweh? Early and often is the only answer to that question. Yahweh answered Jonah. The carnal part of me says why? Jonah did nothing but run, ignore, and disobey Yahweh in this conversation, so why would Yahweh want anything to do with him? Jonah was Yahweh's prophet at that time, and there are many lessons and conversations that need to be had.

Sheol is a place where the dead from earth go to wait for their final destination. Jonah believed that was where he was. We can only imagine the sensation or lack of sensations Jonah was enduring while it was dark and cramped. Jonah cried for help. His cry was not just tears but must have been out of anguish and a place of not understanding the depths of his location. Perception is everything, Jonah perceives that he is in Sheol, the place no one wants to be. How do you get out of Sheol? You cry for help. This must have been a cry from the depths of his heart, and Yahweh heard him. This says that Yahweh will hear you, even in the depth of your sin. Even when you have found the bottom, Yahweh will hear your voice. There is no quitting until you have no more life. Jonah had life, but he did not know where his life was or where he was going, so he perceived the worst was coming his way, and thus the cries. Yahweh heard. He did not turn a deaf ear. He heard Jonah. He will hear you.

2:3

And you threw me into the deep, into the heart of the seas, and the sea currents surrounded me; all your breakers and your surging waves passed over me.

It's odd that Jonah accuses Yahweh of throwing him into the deep. Was it Yahweh's choice to run? Was it Yahweh's decision to not pray, and was it Yahweh's decision to hate Ninevah? No is the answer to all of those questions. It was Jonah's decision for all those things to happen. So the statement "you threw me into the deep" is false. What have you blamed Yahweh for—drugs, drinking, bad relationship choices, things you seek on your phone or computer, or anything you are addicted to?

Perception becomes reality. Jonah believes that he is in the depths of the sea and that there is no returning from there. He perceives that there is no return from this place, as many who are deep in sin believe. The heart of the sea is in the middle of all that is surrounding you as you go deeper into addiction or improper friendships, but you do not see your way out.

Did you ever just want a hug? Jonah received a hug

from the sea as it surrounded him. That was the beginning of how he saw it was going to end. The currents of the sea are stronger than we know, and they are more powerful than we could walk or swim away from. With the water growing, surging, and breaking over Jonah, he sees that his chances of survival get smaller and smaller. We go to the beach to watch the waves, and we are at peace. Jonah is in the waves and is terrified. The waves are breaking over him as they push him in the direction Yahweh wants him to go. This is not a gentle push; it is a shove with all the power needed to move Jonah in the direction Yahweh requires of him.

Our sin passes over us as a reminder of how wrong we were to decide to follow our own desires. Our sin does not want to let us go. It wants to hit us and remind us that we are not what we need to be. That is where Jonah is, remembering that he should have just gone to Nineveh and not tried to run away. There are many "if only" thoughts, but those thoughts mean nothing because you did not do what was asked. The new thought needs to be this: What do I do from this time forward?

2:4

And I said, "I am banished from your sight; how will I continue to look on your holy temple?"

Jonah continues to attempt to admonish Yahweh for the predicament he has put himself in. "I am banished"—I cannot do what I want to do, I am not able to go where I want, and these things I say I want to do because I should do them I cannot do because of you. The reality is that because of me, I cannot do the things I want to do. How often do I have negative consequences because of me? Always. Those consequences often lead me to be stuck looking up at my sins, wondering how it got this far and how I can get back to where I should not have left to begin with. Jonah wants to be in Yahweh's sight, or so he says. If he wanted to be in Yahweh's sight, he should have done what it takes to not leave the sight of God. Temptation and self-destruction will often lead us from the presence of Yahweh.

This is quite the manipulation attempt on Jonah's part. "How will I continue to look on your holy temple?" It is manipulation because Jonah is saying that he wants to look upon Yahweh, but he is not able to because of the consequence of his actions toward Yahweh. This is like saying, "I would like to do this or that, but . . ." It is the "but" that shows what someone is really wanting to do instead of doing what they need to do. I would like to go to the hospital to visit someone who needs kindness extended to them, but I must do something that has no real benefit to anyone but myself.

Who needs your attention? Who needs your love? Who is missing out on time with you that would benefit from your acting out the fruit of the Spirit? To be able to look upon the temple of Yahweh is a wonderful thing. If that opportunity is taken from us, then it is you who takes that away, not Yahweh. When we miss out on the presence of Yahweh, it is because we have chosen to miss out on what He wants for us.

To use the excuse of my consequences because of my actions is to miss the mark of the prize of the high calling of Yahweh. To say it is because of something else that I cannot do what is needed is to say that Yahweh has taken away from me what I need to follow Him. That is not the correct answer—ever. If you start a reply with "I would but," you are starting the answer wrong.

2:5

The waters encompassed me up to my neck; the deep surrounded me; seaweed was wrapped around my head.

Water is a necessary part of life that may find a way to end our life. We need water for more than we can truly understand completely, but in Jonah's case, it was the potential end of his life. That opens a new fear for Jonah: drowning, surrounded by water without any way to get out. He is beginning to be overwhelmed with the water as only his head is above the water.

His thoughts at this point must have been this: I should have done what Yahweh asked me to do, then I would not be up to my neck in trouble. No matter what he did at this point, all he had was a head above the pending doom. The deep surrounded him. He could not see what was to come from there, just that it was all around him. What is in the deep? What could be coming to get him? And what gets him is the seaweed wrapped around his head. Of all the things that could cause death, he notes that the plant is his hat.

Though that seems to be a complaint, I would think that a hat, even of seaweed, would be better than the scorching sun.

When should Jonah have turned back and followed Yahweh? When will you turn back and follow Yahweh? When will you not just stop running from Yahweh but run to Him with the plan of following His plan for your life? Do you go to church? That's good, but it's not great because that is not what is asked of you. What is asked of you is to have the fruit of the Spirit. Do you love your neighbor as yourself, even the one who plays loud music, the one who drinks too much, or the one with a messy yard? Which one do you love? If you don't love all of these, you are doing it wrong. If you are doing it wrong, then you need to see what is wrapped around your head that needs to be removed with the plan to follow Yahweh. Things that are wrapped around your head that will pull you down are social media, not liking one person for whatever reason, and excuses of self-indulgences that keep you from church and wrapped up in the unnecessaries of life. Jonah was wrapped in the seaweed of himself that was going to kill him, or so he thought at that moment.

2:6

I went down to the foundations of the mountains; the Underworld—its bars were around me forever. But you brought up my life from the pit, Yahweh my God.

"I went down to the foundations of the mountains"— the vastness of the mountains is telling you that how to believe you are at the foundations would be feeling the pressure and depths of the world upon you. We see a building and know the foundation is large and strong because of what it is holding up. Think of skyscrapers, for example. What we see is enormous, but what we don't see is what is strong enough to hold up what needs to be held up. Mountains are larger overall than most buildings with a foundation that is not able to be grasped. Here is Jonah realizing that his poor choices have put him in this place of desolation and depth that he is not able to get out of on his own. His perception is that the strength of the location he is against is unable to be moved.

The Underworld—could this be Jonah's perception of hell? Could this be his thought on what Sheol would be? I'm not sure, but I *am* sure it is not what Hollywood has made it out to be—you know, shady people selling and buying on the streets, all dark and dingy. From the brief description, we could assume that Jonah would have preferred to be at the Hollywood version of the Underworld. "Its bars were around me forever"—it seems to me that he either felt the ribs of the large fish or could see them at some point. Time must have felt like it would not end. He was deep in his sin and could not see a way out, which made time stand still for him.

But you, oh Yahweh, you brought me back, you gave me life again, and you did not leave me in the depths of my despair. Jonah was in a pit, and as far as he knew, he did not have a path or direction to get out—but for Yahweh, until Yahweh decided to bring him back. How long did it take for Jonah to acknowledge Yahweh his God? How long will it take before you acknowledge Yahweh God is the only thing that can bring you back from the point of no return? "Yahweh my God" is the answer. When you are in the bars of your sin at the depths of hell, the only thing that will help is Yahweh my God.

2:7

When my life was ebbing away from me, I remembered Yahweh, and my prayer came to you, to your holy temple.

Jonah felt his life sliding away. It was going at such a pace that he did not see a way to stop it. It was going away faster because of his poor choice. To know you are going to die is typical, but to know when you are going to die is not common. Jonah believes he knows the end of his life has arrived. The word *ebbing* here is quite the word choice. Jonah felt a period of decline in his life and his inability to come back from the damage. His physical damage was self-inflicted because of his choice—his choice to not listen to Yahweh's plan for his life. What plan for your life did you walk away from?

Oh! Wait! There is one who can help me. Then Jonah remembered Yahweh, as if he could forget Yahweh. Remembering Yahweh should have been the first thing he did. To finally remember Yahweh tells us that his mind was not in the right place. Why does it take hard times to remember

Yahweh? This is not to say that forgetting Yahweh puts us in this place or that having problems is because we forget Yahweh, but we need to ask, *Why does it often take so long to remember Yahweh?* Often the problems we have are self-inflicted, so we need to be willing to seek Yahweh to help us get out of those self-inflicted problems. When we are suffering because of something that is not self-inflicted, we should reach out to Yahweh even faster because we do not understand what put us where we are. Our prayers that are earnest do reach Yahweh. They do make it to His ears, and He will address them as He sees fit and in His time. In the case of Jonah, it was three days later.

"My prayer came to you"—Jonah knew Yahweh heard him, and that is how we get to read this series of events that happened. If Yahweh had not heard him, there would be no book of Jonah. If there was no Jonah, would we be inserting your name for Jonah's? Do your prayers make it to Yahweh? If they do not, why not? What have you done or not done that would make our heavenly Father not want to hear your prayers and answer you in your time of stress, self-inflicted or not? Our prayers are intended for Yahweh, always. Reaching Yahweh is where we need our prayers to go. We want them to get there so we can make sure we are on His side of everything. Attempting to understand the glory of Yahweh's holy temple is beyond our comprehension because of our finite minds. The most beautiful thing here is nothing compared to the beauty of any part of heaven.

2:8

Those who worship vain idols forsake their loyal love.

"*Those* who worship vain idols"—did Jonah not worship the vain idol of himself? What vain idol do you worship? Is it sexual promiscuity, Facebook, YouTube, yourself, getting those likes, going viral, and more? They are out there and in your face daily, taking your time from what is important: Yahweh and His plan for your life. Do you read the Bible as much as you read your social media posts? Do you care about what Yahweh says about you and life as much as you worry about the latest influencer? Have you prayed as much as you have played that gaming system that takes so much of your time? What have you done before, during, and after your time with Yahweh? All the things we put in front of Yahweh are things that take our loyal love from Yahweh and give it to them—the things that are idols. If you love someone, you show them your love by giving them time. But you do not show Yahweh love with time. You show Him disdain and ignore His love for you. You don't show Him love based on the time that is taken from Him because of your time-sucking idols.

2:9

But I, with a voice of thanksgiving, will sacrifice to you; I will fulfill what I have vowed. Deliverance belongs to Yahweh!

"With a voice of thanksgiving"—should this have been earlier in this conversation? Sure, but it is hard to be thankful when you're in a difficult time. Gratitude for all things is pleasing to the one you are grateful for or because of. When I was a teenager, I loved to go to the skating rink. Since I was young, I did not always have enough money to go, so I asked my dad for some spending money. To be funny, he handed me the smallest amount he had—a quarter or a dollar—which did not go far. I would then say thank you and walk away, I was grateful for whatever he offered. As I walked away, he would call me back to give me what I needed and more. I am sharing that story not to say I always make the right choice but to say that if my earthly father can give me more than I need when I am grateful, then how much more will our heavenly Father do for us as we are grateful for the small things?

Jonah has decided that he will sacrifice to Yahweh. Is this Jonah making a deal with Yahweh to get out of the belly of the fish? It looks like it, but I have hope that Jonah is being genuine in his decision to worship Yahweh. Jonah has realized that he is deep in the depths of his sin and poor decision-making and that there is no other option but to worship Yahweh as needed. Jonah will sacrifice to Yahweh because he knows he is deep in his sin and there is no other way out. He has decided to make a promise—a promise to worship Yahweh in the way that is required.

Jonah has decided to sacrifice to Yahweh. I have decided to follow Jesus, so how do I do that? Jonah had to offer a live sacrifice that died; we offer a dead sacrifice for life. I have decided to give Jesus my everything, so how do I do that?

It is a daily, hourly, moment-by-moment process. When is the last time you actually acknowledged that Jesus is your everything and gave it all to Him—your job, your spouse, your money, your emotions, your social media feed, and so on? Jesus gave His all for you. What are you holding back from Him?

Jonah has made a vow and has taken it back from Yahweh. Now he is offering to give it back to Yahweh because he is in the depths of his sin with no way to turn back. Jonah understands that he cannot rescue himself, and Yahweh is the only way deliverance happens. There are many plans and many paths that will help us be delivered, but Yahweh is the only real way to be permanently rescued. Deliverance is Yahweh's alone.

2:10

And Yahweh spoke to the fish, and it vomited Jonah out on the dry land.

"Yahweh spoke." How many times has Yahweh spoken and miracles happened? It's more than can be numbered. Yahweh spoke on behalf of Jonah and released him from the prison he put himself into because he did not want to follow the plan that was put before him. Yahweh spoke, and the depth of sin Jonah found himself in was removed. All that was required for Jonah to be released from his prison was for Yahweh to speak on Jonah's behalf. Even the sea creatures listen to Yahweh as He speaks. Are you better than the sea

creatures? Yes. Yes is the answer. We have been given domin-
ion over all things on and in the earth.

"Vomit"—not a great topic, but we need to presume that
this was not just a gentle vomit but a projectile vomit. Jonah
was violently projected onto dry land. He skipped all the
water and mud to find dry land. That must have been quite
the trip. Jonah's decision to sin took him to a ship, the ship
took him to the sea, the sea took him to a fish, and the fish
took him back to dry land where he started. Your sin takes
you to pleasure, pleasure takes you to guilt, guilt takes you to
repentance, and repentance takes you back to Yahweh where
you should have stayed. Sin is fun for a moment, but then it
shows its ugly self, and you suffer the consequences of that
sin. If the sin does not kill you, you may be projectile vomited out of the sin. Take that moment and praise Yahweh.
Then find a way to never go back.

CHAPTER 3

3:1

And the word of Yahweh came to Jonah a second time, saying,

"The word of Yahweh"—that is amazing on its own. The word came to Jonah in such a way that there was no mistake that it was from Yahweh. When is the last time you heard from Yahweh and had no mistake that it was from Him? If you have not heard from the Holy Spirit, you need to ponder your salvation. Not only did the word of Yahweh come to Jonah at one time, but we also see that it came a second time. It would be amazing to follow Yahweh from the first time we hear from Him. Often it takes us a few times to listen and follow. Jonah went extremely away from Yahweh, so the path to get him back on track had to be extreme. Now we are at the point of a second time Jonah hears from Yahweh. What measures does Yahweh need to take to get your attention? Next, we see what the second attempt from Yahweh was.

3:2

"Get up! Go to Nineveh, the great city, and proclaim to it the message that I am telling you."

"Get up!" That was direct and to the point as it needs to be. I hear you. You are not broken. Dust yourself off, clean up your clothes, and look as presentable as possible. When you fall, and you will, this is what you need to remember to do— get up! Getting up is the first step in getting moving because if you are on the floor, you are not moving. Go to Nineveh, the place you ran from, the place you despise, the place you are afraid of, the place that you . . . well, whatever excuse you use to not go to the place Yahweh has directed you to go. Yahweh calls it a great city. We would presume that it is great in size and not so great in the quality of people. How big that city was is not as important as following the directions you have been given. When we let the overwhelming size of something get in the way, we are saying to Yahweh, "I don't care what you want; I am not following your plan."

Proclaim the message you are told. So many thoughts, times, and emotions can come from this. When was the last time you were directed to speak but did not? Were you sitting in a meeting when you had the answer but thought you were not respected enough to answer it? Were you in church with your heart pounding and the words in your mind but not the courage of heart to speak the truth? These come to mind because I was one who dealt with both regrettable moments, and now I do not know how someone else's life might have been better if I had just spoken up.

Jonah does not have any question about what he is to say. Yahweh will tell him specifically what he needs to say. Jonah is even told in this verse that it will be Yahweh's message. You may think that would make it easier to say what is needed, but Jonah reminds us that we still have a free will to try not to say what needs to be said to the ones who are lost. The lost are not always non-Christians. There are some Christians who are confused and lost in their lives, not seeking truth but seeking self-desires.

Thought of the moment: Did Jonah hear this from Yahweh as he was flying through the air with his seaweed hat after being projectile vomited out of the fish? Or did Yahweh wait until Jonah landed to discuss the next steps? Life does seem to slow down when a traumatic event happens. How many promises did you make in the moment you were overwhelmed with something, just to end up saying just kidding or I did not mean that. God, if you give me the job that I think is my dream job I will go back to church, but now you still do not know the color of the pews. What will it take for Yahweh to get your attention? It took a fish to get Jonah's attention. That is dramatic.

3:3

So Jonah got up and went to Nineveh according to the word of Yahweh. Now Nineveh was an extraordinarily great city—a journey of three days across.

Jonah got up. So what if he got up? Thankfully, that is not how it was written. "So Jonah got up and went"—as in he finally followed the directions he was given. So I finally followed Yahweh's dream for me to be a teacher, I finally started going back to church, and I followed through with my promise to Yahweh in my time of trouble. And Jonah went to the place that was not far from his starting point—finally following the word of Yahweh.

To understand the extraordinary greatness of Nineveh, we need to understand that the greatness of Nineveh does not mean lovely and kind, but rather enormous. Their mode of transportation was walking, and we see that it was a three-day walk across the city. If I was to travel by car for three days, I would go from Maine to California with time to spare. This city was large and overwhelming in the grandness of all that could be seen and done, but we must also remember that this city was evil. Knowing that Jonah did not want to be there in the first place, it must have felt even more daunting for him to try to begin the process of telling the people to repent of their sins.

3:4

And Jonah began to go into the city a journey of one day, and he cried out and said, "Forty more days and Nineveh will be demolished!"

Jonah began; he began the dreaded thing that he did not want to do in the beginning of this narrative. He began to walk the walk of one who was defeated. His appearance was a sight that would get people's attention—pale from the digestion his body had gone through, a seaweed hat, scrapes from the landing after being projectile vomited, and dejected because he had to do what he should have done from the beginning.

The journey of a thousand days starts with a day. Day one for Jonah as he was crossing the great city was a day of crying out. We can assume that he cried out because he did not want to be there, and this was the fastest way to get his task completed. The cry was one that not many heard before, especially in this exceedingly great city. "Forty more days and Nineveh will be demolished!" There is nothing about how to fix this situation. This city is going down. Forty days and all you know is going to be gone. Forty days and what you know will be just a memory for someone else. "Demolished"—that is rather final in the conversation. Nothing comes back from being demolished and is ever the same again. Jonah saw the face of Yahweh and decided to run. This exceedingly great city does not see the face of Yahweh and is told they will be destroyed. Soon we will see the decision they make when Jonah tells them their great city will be demolished.

3:5

And the people of Nineveh believed in God, and they proclaimed a fast and put on sackcloth—from the greatest of them to the least important.

Well, what happened at Nineveh was nothing but amazing and a blessing that could only come from Yahweh. They believed in God. The angels celebrate over one that comes to

Jesus. Can you imagine the celebration over a city coming to Yahweh? They believed in God, not gods. What a transformation that must have happened! It is interesting that they did not have to go to church to transform, they did not have to have classes to transform, and they did not have to learn specific Bible verses. They just believed. That tells me that we may overcomplicate many things. The Holy Spirit is the one who moves, and we are the ones who need to be able to be moved to the place we are called to be. Jonah had to get up and go. He had tried to go somewhere else, but eventually he got up and went to Nineveh. Yahweh may have had an overall plan for Jonah; we are not sure at this moment.

The people of Nineveh proclaimed a fast and put on sackcloth. They did not wait for someone to tell them what to do; they did the right thing without directions. They knew they were acting wrong and needed to do things right. If you know the right thing to do and choose not to do it, you are wrong in your actions. However, if you do not know what is right because of your surroundings, are you still responsible? Yes! There is no valid reason to do what is wrong except for fulfilling your own lust and desires. The people of Nineveh knew only wrong. When they were confronted with right, they changed, proclaimed a fast, and put on sackcloth. It is awesome that there was no need for leadership to tell them to do the right thing; they just did it. Why don't you seek to do what is right when you are told you are wrong? If you don't, my guess is because you have selfish ambitions, are too proud, or see no benefit.

The fast and the sackcloth proclamation was for all, from the greatest to the least, from the wealthiest to the poorest. All were included, which is the way it needs to be. There is no reason for us to wait for the leaders of the nation to make a decision to do what is right. We should seek to do what is right no matter our status or ability. If we cannot do what is right when we are the least, how will we do what is right when we have the power to make decisions?

3:6

And the news reached the king of Nineveh, and he rose from his throne and removed his royal robe, put on sackcloth, and sat in the ashes.

With no all-knowing social media or news station, the news reached the king of Nineveh. Take yourself to the time before all the information-sharing abilities that we have. That is how the news got to the king. We don't know the length of time it took to get the news from Jonah's shouting to the ears of the king; we just know it got there. This was so important to the king that he rose from his throne. It was something so important that the king found himself unable to continue to sit there. He knew this was important. There is nothing more important than learning that you are a sinner in need of a Savior.

The king had the best of the best—the best-feeling, the softest, the most comfortable, and the best looking—yet he decided to remove all his royal clothing to put on sackcloth.

That would be like taking off your most comfortable sitting-around-the-house clothes and putting on a burlap sack. Quite frankly, I am not interested in that, but this news was so important that the king wanted to set an example for all his people. And the king did not stop there. He also sat in the ashes. He humbled himself to show that he was as the people were—sinners—and he needed to change because of the evil that was throughout the city of Nineveh. Showing that he was as dirty as the citizens meant he understood that he was part of the problem and wanted to be part of the solution. How many leaders, including those in churches, show themselves to be part of the people and not better than the rest of them? How many follow what needs to be done to save the city, state, or nation? Not many.

3:7

And he had a proclamation made, and said, "In Nineveh, by a decree of the king and his nobles: 'No human being or animal, no heard or flock, shall taste anything! They must not eat, and they must not drink water!'"

And the king of a city full of sin and brutal violence made a proclamation. It all started when Yahweh told Jonah to go to Nineveh. Then Jonah proclaimed their sin to the people of Nineveh. Now we have the ruler of Nineveh proclaiming to the people of the city.

Those who are Christ-followers are called to fast and pray. Here we have the king making all the people and livestock fast and pray. The decree was made by the king and his nobles, and all the politicians agreed that this was right. When is the last time you saw all the leaders agree on something? This says that the proclamation from Jonah was taken to heart by all, and thus all will be destroyed.

It is worth noting that the king did not leave anyone or anything out of this decree. That is how laws should be written—simple and to the point. All things included in the decree, including not eating or drinking, seem extreme, but if you are going to do something, you must do it well and right. The words *shall not* and *must not* need to be understood because they are the ones dictating what is next. Shall not taste anything is to the point; nothing is to be on your tongue or entering your mouth. They must not eat, which is in itself demanding and commanding by the authority of the king. They are not to eat but also not drink water. Wow! How harsh that sounds. But the reality is that they learned of the evil they put upon others. When we learn how evil we are, we need to be repentant just as much. That is what we see happening here.

3:8

And the human beings and the animals must be covered with sackcloth! And they must call forcefully to God, and each must turn from his evil way and from the violence that is in his hands.

The human must be covered in the most uncomfortable clothing they can wear, and the animals are included in this covering. Going from silk and soft clothing to burlap sack would make me want to cry out to Yahweh. Including the animals seems odd, but we see in the New Testament that we are told to "go into all the world *and* preach the gospel to all creation" (Mark 16:15). That looks like a way to make sure all are participating in what is required for the relationship with Yahweh to be repaired.

The next sentence includes all calling forcefully to God. Do you call forcefully to God? I will call to Yahweh, but I do not know what it is to call forcefully to Yahweh. The king is calling for repentance of the whole city to Yahweh. The people are called to turn from evil. He did not say anything specifically evil but rather all evil. There is no need for a list here. You know what you are doing that is evil, so stop it. The king did not end at evil; he included violence that is in the hands of the people. There are many things that are violent to others, and that is what they needed to leave behind. The king knew all the evil and violence. He had probably participated in the evil and violence and therefore knew what needed to be said and done.

3:9

Who knows? God may relent and change his mind and turn from his blazing anger so that we will not perish.

All are told that they need to do as commanded because "who knows?" Who does know the outcome of an event except for Yahweh? That brings up this: If we do not change our way, then Yahweh knows the outcome. But when we do change as directed, then our outcome will be the desired outcome. When you are on a path that is leading to destruction and you are given a different path, are you strong enough to follow Yahweh or weak enough to continue the easy path to destruction? God may change His mind; He has in times past. Remember that God is who He was, is, and is yet to come—not like the ghosts of Christmas but as the creator of all we have and are.

We look at Yahweh in the Old Testament and see the destruction that had to happen because of disobedience and corruption. I do not want to be the next in the lineup of destruction for not changing as needed or as directed. To be in the path of destruction because of disobedience is to perish. To change our ways to follow the Creator of all is to put us on the path of eternal life. I do not wish to perish. I have to assume that no one wants to perish. But when we continue down the path of destruction, we will perish.

3:10

And God saw their deeds—that they turned from their evil ways—and God changed his mind about the evil that he had said he would bring upon them, and he did not do it.

How far do you believe Yahweh is from us? This verse says He is not far. God saw their deeds. He did not get a report or see something on social media; He saw. He had a direct view of what they were doing, just as He has with you now. God saw their deeds, as we saw in the previous verse. He was, is, and will always be the same. They turned. When was the last time you turned? When is the last time you listened to someone with a better map and turned your direction? It is not too late to turn.

The people in Nineveh were happy in their evil, but they turned when someone with a better map showed up. Yahweh changed His mind because they had the ability to turn, and they turned. He did not bring His wrath upon them.

The evil that Yahweh could bring is nothing compared to the evil that we can and have done to each other. Because they turned, He did not destroy them. There is a theme in this verse. What do you need to turn from to not see the destruction of Yahweh? Yahweh has a plan for all. Will you follow His map or your own? Following your own map leads to a place like Nineveh. You can change from that map and follow Yahweh's map that leads away from destruction. God does change His mind and His plan. It is up to us to make sure it is changed in the right direction.

CHAPTER 4

4:1

And this was greatly displeasing to Jonah, and he became furious.

This was a great thing that the lives of all in the city were spared because they listened to Jonah, a man of God. Yahweh changed His mind because the people of the city—from the king to the pauper—changed their minds. This thing that was amazing was greatly displeasing to Jonah. Why? Why would an amazing thing be so displeasing? It seems to me that Jonah hated those people who lived in Nineveh.

Who do you hate? What nation do you want to all die and go to hell? What city do you think needs to be destroyed? What family is evil according to you? What person do you think needs to be murdered? The name that comes to your mind makes you no better than Jonah. He became furious—not just upset or bothered, but furious. What right does he, do you, have to be furious? These people that some are wishing evil upon are made in the image of God.

4:2

And he prayed to Yahweh and said, "O Yahweh, was this not what I said while I was in my homeland? Therefore, I originally fled to Tarshish, because I knew that you are a gracious and compassionate God, slow to anger and having great steadfast love, and one who relents concerning calamity."

Jonah prayed to Yahweh. Should he have not been doing that from the beginning? Prayer lines us up with Yahweh, not Him with us. Jonah knew this was going to happen. It was a great thing that happened. Jonah knew it so well that he tried to flee to Tarshish that was 2,500 miles away. Jonah knew Yahweh was so good that he tried to be as far away as he could. That is how much he hated the people of Nineveh. Jonah knew Yahweh to be the gracious God that He is, and because of that, Jonah ran. Yahweh's compassion and slowness to anger are what made Jonah know that Nineveh was going to be okay overall.

At the end of this verse, we see that Yahweh does not want calamity but restoration. That is what Yahweh wants for all—restoration not calamity—but to have restoration, you must come to Him and ask for forgiveness. You must acknowledge your sin and turn from it. That is the way to not have the destruction coming your way. For Yahweh to change His mind you need to change your mind as well. How often have you said, "If God will do this or that, I will do that or this?" Do you find that to be pretentious? Your child or employee comes to you wanting something. Do they have anything they can barter with? You have the power. They are seeking your power, and they will offer to clean up for money or more time to play. So you give in and give them what they want. However, they do not follow through. Then you are the one who has lost, and they gained all the power. That is how we treat Yahweh. If you will give me that money, I will go to church or share with others. Then when you chose to not go, it tells something awful about your integrity. Your calamity should be coming, but Yahweh is so amazing that you do not get all you have coming to you in the form of punishment.

4:3

And so then, Yahweh, please take my life from me, because for me death is better than life!

When was the last time you were so angry you wanted to die? That is Jonah now. He was not begging for his life; he was begging for his death. That comes back to who do you hate so much that you want them to die, or if they do not die you want to die yourself? Do you have the right to hate anyone that much? Death is never the answer—the death of the one hated or the death of self. Death is never the answer. Yahweh had many opportunities to take Jonah's life, but that did not happen because Yahweh was not done with him. Yahweh could have taken Jonah's life at any time in any way, but He was not done teaching Jonah or us what we all need to know. Jonah claims that death is better than life. How is death better? With life you still have time to change your actions and emotions to align with Yahweh, but with death it is over. Jonah had the opinion of finality; Yahweh had the better opinion of continuation. Continuation is always better until it cannot be anymore. It's Yahweh's choice, not ours.

4:4

And Yahweh said, "Is it right for you to be angry?"

This continuing conversation between Jonah and Yahweh is like ours. We have an opinion, and Yahweh says we are asking for the wrong thing. Yahweh always has the right question and answer. Do you have the right to be angry at anyone or anything? Sure, we will have frustrations and want to do this or that, but we cannot because of other things that need to be done. We can get angry about a person or a group of people doing what is wrong, but acting out in anger is not the right answer. Ephesians 4:26–27 says, "Be angry and do not sin; do not let the sun set on your anger, nor give place to the devil." These verses have been included to show that anger does happen and that it is okay, but we need to not let it turn into sin. Sinning gives way to the devil winning a place in your heart and mind. So do you have the right to be angry? No, but I am so selfish that I am angry, and that is all I want and need to know.

4:5

And Jonah went out from the city and sat down east of the city, and he made for himself a shelter there. And he sat under it in the shade, waiting to see what would happen with the city.

Imagine Jonah's thoughts: "I did what I was told, now let's see the city fall. I am going to watch from over there." Jonah went out and did what he needed to do, even after all the struggle it took to get him there. His attitude was frustration and even anger. He made a shelter with the plan of watching destruction. The shade was good enough to give him a comfortable place to stay and chill as Nineveh fell into darkness, or so he hoped. What do you want to happen to the ones you hate? What do you want to happen to those who repent because of the love of Yahweh? Do you want to sit and watch them become nothing, or do you want them to succeed? I know that many will say, "I want them to succeed," but under your breath you want them to fail and be destroyed. That makes you the same as Jonah. What is your shelter, your house, your office, your car, or even your bed as your spouse may be the one you hate? Are you waiting to see what will come of the one you hate? I hope it's like watching for a pot to boil that does not boil.

4:6

And Yahweh God appointed a plant, and he made it grow up over Jonah to be a shade over his head, to save him from his discomfort. And Jonah was very glad about the plant.

Yahweh God did another thing. Note that this is Yahweh God, not a god. The difference is imperative to the full conversation. Yahweh God can do as He desires, but a god with a small *g* cannot do anything unless it is deemed possible by Yahweh God. Seeds do not do anything unless it is time for them to do what is required of them.

We can grow plants from seeds for food, shade, or houses. Here, Yahweh appointed a plant. He made this plant grow where it was needed and to be as large as it was required. Yahweh made this plant happen just for Jonah. It was not for anyone else or for any other time. Yahweh knew what Jonah needed and provided it, even though Jonah did not follow Yahweh's original plan. This plant was used to save Jonah from discomfort. It was a blessing Jonah did not deserve. Jonah was very pleased with an item that was for him from Yahweh. I would also be pleased with something that would help lessen my discomfort. All this is about a plant. The plant was what Jonah wanted and needed, and he would not have had it if it weren't for the grace and mercy of Yahweh God.

4:7

So God appointed a worm at daybreak the next day, and it attacked the plant, and it withered.

A worm—not an army of worms or a few worms but just a worm—was appointed by Yahweh. It seems ironic that a worm has the ability to do what Yahweh says better than a human. We have free will; we use it horribly. The worm was sent in the morning to start the process of killing the plant. The worm was so relentless in the attack of the plant that the plant withered, leaving Jonah without the shade he so desired and needed. This is the plant that Jonah was so happy to have. It's like getting your favorite thing as a gift and having it taken away from you the next day. It was a you-got-a-new-fancy-phone-and-then-dropped-it-in-the-ocean type of disappointment. What is Jonah to do now?

4:8

And when the sun rose, God appointed a scorching east wind, and the sun beat down on Jonah's head and he grew faint. And he asked that he could die and said, "My death is better than my life!"

The worm killed the plant before the rising of the sun. The sun is coming into view, and soon it will be warm. Yahweh was not done teaching Jonah that he had issues that needed to be resolved. Now He sends a scorching east

wind. I have been mowing lawns for a few summers at this
point, and heat is no joke. There is never enough water to
keep me hydrated. You might think there was relief because
of the wind, but this was not a normal wind. It was a
scorching east wind that would cause burning on your skin.
There was no comfort from this wind. The sun arrives and
adds to the pain and suffering as it beats down on Jonah's
flesh. The heat was so bad that Jonah grew faint. Being in
the sun and heat so much makes you dehydrated, and there
is nothing that can ease the suffering from the sun and a
scorching wind.

At this point, life is grim for Jonah. It is so grim that
he is wishing death upon himself. Sadness and depression
take over. That is not a surprise. He had just seen a whole
city worship Yahweh for the first time, which should have
been an amazing moment in his life. For Jonah to believe
that his death would be better than his life says that he
does not care about anyone or anything except himself.
Wanting to die before it is your time is a selfish desire, and
no one should ever want to die before Yahweh calls them
home.

4:9

*So God said to Jonah, "Is it right for you to be angry about the
plant?" And he said, "It is right for me to be angry enough to die!"*

Yahweh spoke to Jonah again. Again? Yes, again. Yahweh could have been upset with Jonah and said nothing to

him; however, Yahweh is slow to anger and does not stop talking just because we make bad choices. When is the last time you heard from Yahweh? If it has been a while, you need to go back and see what you can do to get back to listening to His voice and not your own. Is it right for you to be angry? Sometimes, but in Jonah's instance, what was he angry about? He was angry about the plant being eaten, not the fact that thousands of souls were on their way to hell and he did not care. What is your plant? Is it television time, phone time, an adulterous relationship, games, work, busyness, sickness, hurt, and so on? You know what your plant is. You know how to deal with your plant. Why do you let it live? The irony is that the worm did what Jonah should have done—destroyed the plant that was in the way of following Yahweh.

Jonah's anger was so great that he wanted to die. He did not want to repent, and he did not want to see the best. He wanted to die. What has made you so angry that you wanted to die? Was it the loss of a loved one, loss of a game, or loss of a bet? The only rights we have are the ones given to us by Yahweh. Our right to die is in His hands, not ours. Our anger may take us there emotionally, but that is no reason to desire to die. We need to make sure our actions lead our emotions and not our emotions lead actions. Often emotions are wrong and need adjusted to match what is really happening.

4:10

But Yahweh said, "You are troubled about the plant, for which you did not labor nor cause it to grow. It grew up in a night and it perished in a night!"

Obviously, Jonah was upset about the plant that died—nothing else that we can see. Yahweh calls Jonah out for being upset about the plant. How humbling that must have been. You have been called out, and what did you do when you were told you were wrong? Did you get angrier, lie to make yourself better, or allow the humbling to happen? It is curious that Jonah's anger was over a plant, not over the lives of those in the city of Nineveh. Jonah did not do anything for the plant to come up; he had nothing to do with its arrival. Jonah had no emotional or labor attachment to the plant, yet he was upset that it did not stay. The plant came up in a night and then was taken in a night. It was there and gone faster than most things that are created. If our life is a vapor, the life of this plant was nothing. What in your life is so short that you don't remember it in a week or a month? It is your plant, the thing you really did not have anything to do with but were blessed with and is now gone.

4:11

"And should I not be concerned about Nineveh, the great city, in which there are more than one hundred and twenty thousand people who do not know right from left, plus many animals?"

Yahweh continues. Should He be concerned about Nineveh? Yes, is the fast and easy answer. Who is Yahweh concerned about that you do not like or care about? Is it your neighbor or co-worker that you do not like? Is it your waiter, the person who is not driving well, or the person who is not religious or in your political party? Nineveh was considered a great city for its size—more than 120,000 people. That is more than most cities in the United States. The part we need to take note of is that they were so confused that they did not know right from left, or right from wrong for that matter. Not only was Yahweh concerned about the humans, but He included the animals in His concern. Jonah did not change his position or his anger as far as we can tell. That is not how you need to be.

WRAPPING UP

Yahweh had His man, Yahweh made His plan, Yahweh provided His fish, and Yahweh shared a plant. That can be all we need to understand after some pondering. Diving in further, we see that Yahweh is who He was, is, and will be. Because Yahweh is who He was, He still talks to us, not always audibly but in the way you need Him to talk to you so you will hear Him. Yahweh will be the same tomorrow, so we need to be sure to pay attention to Him today.

This focus on Jonah was not for us to look at Jonah and point our fingers but for us to seek ourselves out and wonder if we are like Jonah. How are you like Jonah? Are you running in another direction? Do you avoid places—inner city, neighbors, mission fields—because you do not like them? Do you have a way to escape? Is it drugs, alcohol, movies, games, or lies you tell yourself? Do you celebrate when someone comes to Christ, or is it just not exciting?

Search yourself and know who you are, but more importantly, find out who you are to Yahweh. When we know who we are to Yahweh, we will know where we need to go and who we need to talk to. This book has been a warning. Do not run so far that you need to have a fish take you to the place you need to be.

www.ingramcontent.com/pod-product-compliance
Lightning Source LLC
Chambersburg PA
CBHW071111090426
42737CB00013B/2567